GORILLAS
Living on the Edge

Andy Rouse

CONTENTS

This book is dedicated to my mother, who sadly passed away shortly before this was published. She could not tell you anything scientific about gorillas and knew nothing about the politics surrounding their conservation. In her view, they were just beautiful animals. Seeing my stories of them in the UK national press always made her laugh, no matter how ill she was feeling. It is this connection between mountain gorillas and us that I hope this book will help to nurture.

My mother had the right idea, to just love mountain gorillas for what they are.

This incredible vista shows the spectacular home for Rwanda's population of mountain gorillas – the Virunga Volcanoes National Park. Spanning three countries (Rwanda, Democratic Republic of Congo and Uganda) the Virungas cover an area of 130 square kilometres. They are all dormant volcanoes, except two in the Democratic Republic of Congo that erupted as recently as 2006.

The highest is Mount Karisimbi at 4,507 metres (14,790 ft) and the oldest is Mount Sabinyo whose sawtooth appearance dominates the range. All are home to groups of mountain gorillas, so come and meet them...

INTRODUCTION

There are four sub-species of gorilla spread across central Africa: the eastern lowland, western lowland, Cross River and, of course, the mountain. Reclusive by nature, the mountain gorilla is found in only two distinct populations. One spans the Virunga Volcanoes National Park in Rwanda, Uganda and the DRC; the second is in the Bwindi Impenetrable Forest, in Uganda. According to the most recent census in 2010, the total population of the mountain gorilla has increased to over 780 individuals; 480 in the Virungas and the remaining 300 in Bwindi. To the casual observer this may not seem like a lot of animals, and the reality is, it is not. The good news is that the population is increasing, but it's a tiny fraction of the original population and there are still too few of them to guarantee their survival. So determined conservation efforts are absolutely essential.

Of course, I am not a scientist or a gorilla expert. I'm just a normal guy who has journeyed many times into the lives of these peaceful great apes. I am passionate, I care and I want you to do the same.

Like most people, the first time I saw gorillas was on television... and my memories of those 'encounters' are hardly positive. In my childhood, the *Planet of the Apes* films gave gorillas a starring role...as violent, unreasonable soldiers. Films like *King Kong*, and more recently *Congo*, have not helped much either by portraying the gorilla as a savage beast. The comic and magazine industries often use gorillas on their covers whenever they need to guarantee a good sale... and typically, the gorillas always look aggressive.

Clearly, gorillas had a PR problem and needed some good TV heroes. The first came in 1979, when Sir David Attenborough sat among mountain gorillas during an episode of his groundbreaking *Life on Earth* series. Even when a silverback charged him, Sir David stayed cool and calm, thus giving us the message that gorillas were to be respected and not feared. In 1988, Sigourney Weaver starred as primatologist Dian Fossey in the Hollywood blockbuster *Gorillas in the Mist.* In 129 minutes of cinematic genius, the world saw the gentle nature of mountain gorillas and how we, as a human race, persecuted and misrepresented them. Gradually, the public perception of gorillas was starting to change for the better, and conservation efforts were gaining more of the support that they needed.

This book is a journey into the life of one of the most endangered, and impressive, animals on the planet...the mountain gorilla.

Being a full-time and self-confessed gorilla fan, I am totally biased of course. Some of you, who have been lucky enough to see gorillas in the wild, will readily agree with me. Others will have the nagging thought that gorillas are terrifying, dangerous beasts.

Gorillas are gentle, peace loving, highly intelligent, family-orientated animals that have long been the subject of appalling persecution and misinformation. How we can treat a creature that shares 98% of our genes in such a way beggars belief. With *Gorillas: Living on the Edge*, I hope to change some of these misconceptions and hopefully, win the gorillas a few more friends. After all, this endangered ape needs all the friends it can get.

Gorillas: Living on the Edge, is more than just another gorilla book. It doesn't dwell on the past but looks instead to a future where we still share the planet with mountain gorillas. It is not only a celebration of the life of the mountain gorilla, but also the rejuvenation of Rwanda and its people. Rwanda is a name that conjures up immediate memories of the appalling genocide in 1994 and instantly gives this beautiful country a stigma that it doesn't deserve. A week before publishing this book, I had a spectacular mountain gorilla picture story published in the UK and international press. I just happened to be in a London pub that very day and overheard people at one table discussing the story. After introducing myself, they asked where I had taken the pictures. After I replied "Rwanda" there was a moment of silence after which one person said, "Oh, it's dangerous there, you must be very brave". It was a sentiment shared by the others. This is not the first time I have encountered this belief about Rwanda; just like the mountain gorillas, it suffers immensely from misconceptions.

Like everyone, I have watched the films and read the books, but until you see and experience Rwanda for yourself, you have no real idea how alive this country is. Personally, I see Rwanda as a friendly, vibrant country with people who always wear a smile. Sure, it has had its well-documented troubles, but the country has dealt with the legacy of its past and now looks to the future. Rwanda cares about its people and it cares about its mountain gorillas too.

In this resource and commodity-driven world, mountain gorillas will only survive by finding a way to pay for themselves. It may be romantic to think that animals are conserved for their good looks alone. However, the reality is very different. In Rwanda, only 130 square kilometres of prime mountain gorilla habitat remains on the steep slopes of the Virunga Volcanoes. Unfortunately, it is not only prime habitat for mountain gorillas but also for human exploitation. The pressure on these slopes is enormous and, in this densely populated corner of Africa, this can only get worse. So while conservation measures against poaching and other such activities are vital, they must go hand-in-hand with the need to involve local communities. Simply speaking, local people need to see the benefit from mountain gorillas for themselves.

Gorillas: Living on the Edge, is a book with a simple theme. Passion.

Through these pages, I hope to take you on an unforgettable and emotional journey into the world of the mountain gorilla. I hope it will show you the incredible power of these gentle giants combined with heart-rending moments of tenderness. Youngsters will look out at the world from within the safety of their mother's embrace, while their older siblings will romp and play in their jungle home.

The love that I have for Rwanda and its mountain gorillas is laid bare in these pages for you all to see.

I am not alone in my passion, as one person, Will Bolsover, has accompanied me on this journey from day one. As Managing Director of World Primate Safaris, Will shares my views and passions about mountain gorillas, and has organised all my tours to see them. We have decided that our contribution to mountain gorilla conservation is to support sustainable tourism by bringing as much money into the Rwandan economy as possible. We leave the science to researchers and the politics to the NGOs; our focus is purely on supporting sustainable tourism. Between us, we have brought over US$500,000 into the Rwandan economy via mountain gorilla tourism, taking many people to see these wonderful apes over the years. At the end of this book, Will shares his thoughts on the benefits and the drawbacks of using tourism for conservation; it is a compelling read.

As well as raising awareness of mountain gorillas and Rwanda, *Gorillas: Living on the Edge*, will make a direct contribution to gorilla conservation. We will donate 25% of all profits from the sales of this book, on a quarterly basis, to mountain gorilla-orientated conservation projects in Rwanda. One recipient will be the Mountain Gorilla Veterinary Project, which you will read about later; others will include education and local community projects. Both Will and I are determined that we can make a difference to this great ape and the journey starts right here.

Gorillas: Living on the Edge, is a book of hope for the future. Mountain gorillas cannot survive on their own. They will probably always need our protection. In order to guarantee the survival of gorillas for generations to come, we need to destroy all misconceptions about the gorilla as an aggressive, terrifying ape. It is not! The gorilla is one of our closest relatives and shares 98% of its DNA with us. It is our wild brother on this planet. It will survive if we really want it to and help it to do so.

Gorillas have to be worth more alive than dead. Rwanda has recognised this and has developed one of the most successful sustainable ecotourism models in the world. This is proving absolutely critical in efforts to protect the mountain gorilla. Revenue from tourism is not only used for gorilla protection but also to fund local community projects such as schools and tourism initiatives. In short, the locals benefit from the tourists and consequently, it is in their own interest to protect the gorillas and their habitat. A win-win situation. There is no doubt that sustainable ecotourism is a major contributor to the increase in the mountain gorilla population. In fact, it is a vital component of their continued growth and of the protection of the Virunga Volcanoes that so many species call home.

MY FIRST TREK

The journey begins

One of the real pleasures of leading gorilla treks is witnessing the emotions when clients see their first wild mountain gorilla. Some cry tears of joy, others stare open mouthed but eventually everyone smiles in the knowledge that they are all sharing something special. I know these memories will stay with them forever; mountain gorillas touch you in this way. I still remember my very first trek. It was a cool misty morning and we stood among groups of boot wearing, gaiter-clad tourists waiting expectantly; the excitement was electric. The park director introduced himself, told us we were to visit the Hirwa group and then introduced us to Olivier who was our guide. In the following ten minutes, I learnt more about mountain gorillas than I ever thought possible. There are seven habituated mountain gorilla groups and eight visitor permits were issued for each group per day. The maximum time allowed with the gorillas was one hour for each group, and even now, this precious time always seems to go too quickly for me.

The trek began and the atmosphere was buzzing; everyone was up for it. Up ahead was the characteristic sawtooth summit of Mount Sabinyo, a ragged old volcano that tells its own story of a violent past. Onwards and upwards we walked, eventually reaching the old stone wall that runs the length of the national park. The contrast is stunning. On one side of the wall is the dense forest that the mountain gorillas call home and on the other side it is a mixture of farmland and pasture. The purpose of the wall is not to keep the gorillas in, but to stop wild buffalo and elephants marauding through the farmland below and destroying the crops. It also serves as a stark reminder of how little mountain gorilla habitat remains.

Once over the wall, the mud started in earnest and soon the group were helping each other up the steep slopes. It is a great leveller as you can be the richest person in the world, but once in the mud, you are the same as everyone else! "Ten minutes to the gorillas" said Olivier and the excitement grew even more. After dumping our rucksacks, we fought our way through some thick bamboo, which did not want to be moved and fought back with a vengeance. Then without warning, we broke into a small clearing and there right in front of me, was the silverback.

He was a huge, seriously impressive animal. I have been close to big animals before of course, very close in fact, but this felt completely different. We had nothing between us; no vehicle, no safety net, nothing. He regarded us with more than a passing interest and he was clearly watching us watching him. Experience told me that I should be nervous, but inside I was completely calm. That is the amazing thing

about gorillas; they exude such incredible calm and peace to all around. The overwhelming emotion I felt was an unreasonable degree of excitement; I felt incredible.

As the hour progressed the gorillas started to spread out a little and by the end, most were asleep. On the way back down, I had time to reflect on the encounter as I slipped and slithered in the mud. I knew it was a special moment for me on so many levels. Although I love all wildlife, mountain gorillas were going to join that special band of animals that I hold closest to my heart. With these animals, I go the extra mile and get involved in their conservation by raising awareness and much needed funds.

For me, that very first silverback has become like an old friend. He is called Muninya, which means "Lucky One", and I have enjoyed watching him and his group flourish. I am now approaching my 50th mountain gorilla trek and for me, every minute of every hour I have spent with the mountain gorillas of Rwanda has been special. In fact, the next minute cannot come soon enough.

SILVERBACKS

Meet the boss

Big, black and mean; that is the historical portrayal of the magnificent silverback or "the Boss". This highly intelligent symbol of pure power is a great leader who shows incredible moments of tenderness and compassion to young and old alike. They are responsible for all aspects of group life, which include deciding where the group feeds each day, security, dispute resolution and reproduction.

The name "silverback" is derived from the wide stripe of silvery-white hairs that grow across the back when the males reach maturity after 10-12 years. At the same time they develop the characteristic domed head too. An average silverback weighs up to 220 kg (400 lbs). This is quite a bit heavier than the biggest American football player and about 1/3rd of the weight of a Mini Cooper car.

The next few pages are my homage to some great silverbacks I have photographed. What better place to start than my favourite. He is Muninya of the Hirwa group. Hot news off the press is that one of his females has just given birth to twins, a very rare event and all of us here wish them the best for the future.

As you read in 'My First Trek', Muninya is the first silverback I ever saw. Known locally as "Lucky One", he has steadily built up his group over the years from just a couple of females. Once females reach maturity, they generally leave their maternal group to avoid inbreeding, so he has certainly benefited from the close proximity of other groups like the 'All Action Kwitonda' and Group 13. This shot was taken during a particularly rainy trek; my friend Lucky isn't a fan of the rain and always has the grumpiest expression when he's wet. Yours truly is equally grumpy in the rain.

Lucky has now developed into a huge silverback, just look at those shoulders. Incredible. Lucky has been kind to me on many occasions, giving me some great photo opportunities. This time was something very special, as a silverback standing on all fours in the clear is a rare occurrence. Lucky just stood there looking at us, it was awe inspiring to say the least; a vision of power just watching over his family.

In his first year of being the dominant silverback, Lucky did have some trouble getting the respect of his females. A silverback leads the group and all should follow without question; if they don't then there is trouble. I watched one morning as Lucky moved off but the females refused to budge and just carried on feeding. He watched them through the canopy, calling a little to encourage them to follow.

Still they refused, so he moved out from the shadows and walked purposefully to where the females were sitting. After a few seconds of silence we heard some muffled noises, which increased greatly in volume to a scream, accompanied by the beating of a chest. A female walked down the path, closely followed by Lucky whose look could only be described as "stern". Clearly he was having none of their rebellion. Satisfied that she was heading in the right direction, he turned and disappeared again in the direction of the females. Soon another female appeared and followed the other. Silverbacks are the undisputed kings of their domain and I guess that Lucky just took a bit of time to get that message across.

Mountain gorilla silverbacks are surprisingly agile despite their enormous bulk, and Lucky demonstrated this when a normal trek turned into a major abseiling experience.

One minute he was in front of us, the next he had disappeared over the edge of a ravine. It was effortless for him, but took all of us 20 minutes to get over the edge as it was almost vertical.

Lucky just sat down and watched us all with interest, as we tried impersonating mountain goats. I am convinced that he spent as much time watching us, as we did watching him.

One of the great characters of the silverback world is the charismatic Kwitonda. Living on the edge of Sabinyo Volcano, he is a very elegant silverback and facially the elder statesman of the mountain gorilla world. He has a very "lived in" face and I have a huge collection of his portraits. His group is called Kwitonda after him, but I refer to them as 'All Action Kwitonda' as they seem to have their fair share of adventures. The group originally lived in the Congo but years of civil strife and gorilla poaching probably made Kwitonda decide to bring the group across to the Rwandan side of the Virungas. I respect him greatly for this and he definitely has had a harder life than most. Despite this, he is a very relaxed silverback. Kwitonda actually means "humble one" and he is certainly that.

I love working with Kwitonda as he is such an accommodating and affable silverback for tourists and photographers alike. Give him space and time and he will always deliver a special experience. With such a characterful face it is tempting to always take close-ups but I love including some of the habitat in my images as it shows the dependence between mountain gorilla and forest.

The biggest mountain gorilla silverback (in terms of weight and bulk) is Guhonda who leads the Sabinyo Group. I was intrigued to see how he compared to Lucky or Kwitonda, both of whom looked perfectly big enough to me. Surely Guhonda wouldn't be that much bigger? I had to find out. The hike to the Sabinyo group passed through a patchwork of agriculture (above). I always feel sorrow that this land has been lost as valuable mountain gorilla habitat, but of course fully understand the needs of people to eat and produce cash crops. The main growth here is for potatoes and pyrethrum, the latter being used as an effective deterrent for mosquitoes.

•••↝ We found Guhonda alone in the forest. First impressions from my group were that he was indeed a very large chap and clearly powerful. I found this out the hard way as he suddenly reached up, grabbed a tree and pulled it down right on top of us. Silverbacks have just awe-inspiring power. I tried afterwards to bend the tree next to it and even with all my weight, I could barely move it!

After removing bits of tree from my head, I rejoined my group and we followed Guhonda through the sizeable hole he had made in the forest. I could hear curses behind as boots were sucked into the gooey undergrowth. Fighting on we found him again a few feet off the ground clinging to a very small tree and staring into the distance. The canopy was too thick to see what he was looking at but something was very interesting to him.

Suddenly he stepped down from the tree and walked in the direction of his stare. The rest of his group followed behind. We waited until the last had passed and tried to follow. After a few minutes we gave up as the vegetation and the mud were just too thick. The show was over, the largest mountain gorilla silverback in the world had granted us a brief audience and now he was on a mission; the outcome we would never know...

Photographing Akarevuro, apprentice silverback from 'All Action Kwitonda', is never without a dull moment. Young developing silverbacks like this are always fun to work with, as you never know what to expect and they have something to prove.

I was photographing one day, when out of nowhere Akarevuro appeared and charged at me through the centre of the group. Peace turned to chaos as gorillas scattered in all directions, fearful that they were the target of the silverback's charge.

Of course there are many more mountain gorilla silverbacks not featured here and over the course of this book you will meet a few more. No matter which group you visit during a mountain gorilla trek, one thing is assured, the silverback is the boss and he knows it.

BAD HAIR DAY

Thank you George

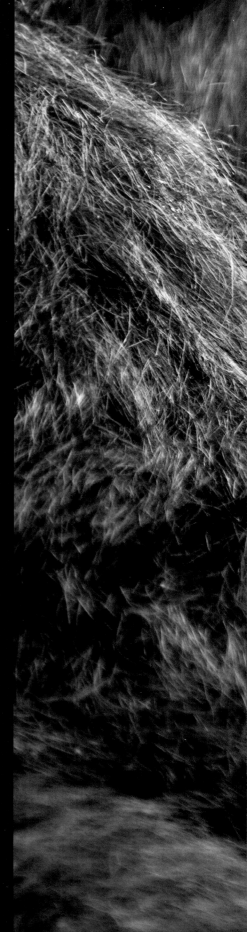

I don't have much to thank George Bush for, but when it comes to mountain gorillas I owe him one. Whilst he was on a state visit to Kigali in 2008 (following on from Bill Clinton's landmark visit in 1998) several of his entourage came to trek with mountain gorillas. Since this was unplanned and unannounced, it meant that they took two of the habituated gorilla groups exclusively for themselves. This left some very unhappy tourists without a gorilla group to visit, including mine, but I knew that the forest department would have another plan; Rwanda values its gorilla tourists. Sure enough, we were told that we would be granted a special visit to one of the research groups. In addition to the habituated groups of mountain gorillas, there are several groups that are used primarily for research observations and see very few tourists. We drove around to the starting point and my first impression was that the path went straight up the mountain. No walking today through endless gentle pastures taking in the air, oh no, this was a fully-fledged slog to heaven. Don't get me wrong, I am no lightweight and love the physical element of my job, but this was a different level of path altogether. After five minutes of gasping for air, the group started to spread out as the steep slope took its toll. I could see why the normal tourists did not do this trek; it was solely for mountain goats! After an hour of making false promises to everyone ("I can see the top, only another five minutes, honestly") we finally reached the wall and collapsed in a heap of complaint. It was the toughest hour of my life.

After a few minutes feeling sorry for myself whilst still lying flat out, I asked the guide how much further it was to the gorillas; he laughed and pointed. There, sitting in a tree above the wall, were three gorillas watching us. The hellish climb was immediately forgotten and the group sprung to life, cameras out and ready to start the visit. The gorillas quietly climbed down and disappeared behind the wall. We scrambled over and immediately saw three females sitting with their youngsters. Quietly we all sat down... and one hour later we were still in the same place...

The reason why? Only the worst example of a bad hair day I think I have ever seen. I have had a few in my time, when I had hair of course, but I could not believe this little guy's shock hair. One of my clients, Giles, remarked that it reminded him of the same hairstyle worn by the late great James Brown. You have to admit that it really is a very bad hair day.

Serious scientific types hate images and commentary like this, as they think that they ridicule gorillas. I completely disagree. Images like this are appealing to the general public and draw people to love gorillas and find out more about them. Connection with the general public is vital for the conservation of any species and especially for the mountain gorilla. If an image like this improves the PR of the mountain gorilla by even a miniscule percentage, then that will help; every little bit helps.

The untold story of these images is how my group behaved towards the gorillas. No one made any sudden movements and everyone stayed still with huge smiles for the whole hour. I have heard tales of some tourists making too much noise and photographers being overly pushy and causing a silverback to charge. My groups have always been so respectful to animals, which I hope comes from a reflection of my own behaviour. On this occasion, there is no doubt that this contributed to the females getting more confident with us and allowing the youngsters to play a little.

Of course they were too young to get up to too much mischief, but still old enough to wake a sleeping mother by jumping repeatedly on her. When this became too much, a large black arm would uncurl itself from a seemingly asleep female and gather up the protesting youngster.

The timeless moment that you see here was just beautiful to watch. The love they showed each other is there for all to see and needs no words.

When siesta time was over and after a lot of stretching and yawning, the females got up and hauled the youngsters onto their backs. My bad hair friend disappeared into the jungle hanging on for dear life. It had been a wonderful experience and all who look at these images smile; they really are a special collection. Kids love them too and they are now the subjects of a children's book entitled *Busy Gorillas*. It is a great feeling knowing that the young generation of one species will inspire another.

ALL ACTION KWITONDA
Coming of age

Every trek with mountain gorillas is different and I never know what to expect. The 'All Action Kwitonda' group, led by the charismatic Kwitonda himself, is always great fun to work with and they specialise in the unexpected. Most days with them are classics, but I never expected to achieve two ambitions in the same hour.

The trek that morning was easy and we found a group of gorillas feeding low down on the mountainside. The dominant silverback, Kwitonda, was sitting against a tree watching us closely as we approached. The trackers stopped, reassured him with a gorilla contact call to which he replied back, and we edged our way into position. I have always been amazed at this communication between the silverback and the guide, because it shows respect on both sides. Once again this demonstrates how close we are to this great ape.

One of the trackers told us that an apprentice silverback, Akarevuro, was sitting in a nice clear area with some females. As a photographer and gorilla-watching addict, this was a good result as sometimes behaviour and "cool stuff" is usually hidden behind vegetation or some insensitively placed trees.

We fought through the bamboo forest and soon found him sitting in a lovely clearing with the haunting mist covered slopes of Sabinyo volcano looming over the tree tops. It was nature's poetry at its finest.

Several females surrounded Akarevuro, which was strange because apprentice silverbacks are meant to watch and not touch. The females seemed very relaxed and calm with Akarevuro; occasionally they groomed him but mostly they just relaxed in the cool, damp air. It was turning out to be a very peaceful morning watching gorillas... but then everything changed...

Without any provocation, Akarevuro fixed on us with a stare, pursed his lips and started to make very gentle hooting sounds. They increased in tempo and Edward, my guide said, "He's going to charge" and made us back off as far as the vegetation would allow. The anticipation was heavy in the damp, morning air...

⟶ ⟶ Overleaf: In an instant, the peaceful vibe was shattered as several hundred pounds of pure muscle stood up and ran straight at us. He beat his fists repeatedly against his chest and crashed powerfully through the bushes, the sound reverberating all around the valley. It was simply an awesome display of Mother Nature's raw power. He covered ten metres in a couple of seconds, but time had no meaning here. I have been charged by a lot of animals in my wild life, but this was completely different. So far I had only experienced the gentle side of a silverback and to see this other side was a complete shock. When he got too close for my lens, I knew that it was time to press the ejector seat button or pull the trap door lever. Luckily he came to a crashing halt a few feet short of me...

Crouching sideways on all fours he looked every inch a powerhouse and slowly, I raised my wider lens. I did not dare make any sudden moves or eye contact. We couldn't move backwards anymore due to the vegetation and I didn't want to hear that chest beating so close! He sat for a while like this, watching intently into the thick bush but occasionally checking on us out of the corner of his eye. Clearly he was watching something but I could not see what. The other gorillas who had scattered during the charge, returned and soon the mood relaxed again. After a few minutes he slowly moved away into the bushes.

This triggered several collective human sighs of relief and excited whispers. It was a total adrenaline rush; the full on charge that I had always wanted to experience and photograph. Before you think it, we were never in any danger of getting hurt. Silverbacks, whilst incredibly powerful, are gentle and highly intelligent. At worst, he could have pushed one of us over but that would have been the exception, and to be honest, several of us were on the verge of falling over from shock anyway. We hadn't done anything to cause it... but something obviously had.

A few minutes later, I found out. Akarevuro was sitting close to a female, looking every inch the dominant silverback that he was growing to be. The female turned her back to him, a clear invitation to mate; she must have been impressed by his show of force. Research has indeed shown that male chest beating, instead of being overtly aggressive, can simply be the male reacting to the presence of a receptive female. I watched as he accepted her invitation...

In my travels I have seen mating of all kinds. Lions mating can be hilarious. Mountain gorilla mating was something totally different. It was tender, loving and for his size he was incredibly gentle. They both made low moaning sounds, it wasn't perverse as you might expect but full of emotion; it was tearfully beautiful. To be honest I felt uncomfortable being there, like I didn't belong, so I turned the camera onto silent and spent most of my time watching.

After a minute she reached round and gripped his arm; the expression of pleasure on her face was priceless and I knew exactly what was happening at that moment...

The mating finished, he moved off to one side to be replaced by two females. In these situations it is easy to be anthropomorphic but there was some communication happening between them. Unfortunately I didn't see anymore as our visiting hour was up, and our guide quietly motioned for us to leave. It had been an amazing morning. The full-on charge had been exhilarating and was in total contrast to the incredible tenderness of the mating; mountain gorillas had surprised me again.

We were all amazed by the boldness of the mating, as Kwitonda (the dominant silverback) must have been within earshot. The dominant silverback tolerates young silverbacks provided they stay away from the group and don't try to mate with any of the females. They are meant to adopt a watching brief and the punishment for anything else is a severe beating or worse. Clearly Akarevuro had different intentions and it was the start of his coming of age. He was reaching the point where he wanted his own females and this would inevitably lead to a confrontation with Kwitonda. It would surely be an interesting year in the 'All Action Kwitonda' group and as it turned out, they would not disappoint...

FACES AND EXPRESSIONS
Watching us watching them

All gorillas... in fact all primates, have wonderfully expressive faces. I guess it is one reason why so many of us feel a connection with them, as many of our facial expressions are identical to theirs. I have seen gorillas frown, look angry, sad, thoughtful, play with their lips and pull all manner of expressions. Several times I have seen Lucky pull a very hacked off and grumpy face whenever it rained. None of these expressions are accidental; they are deliberate acts by a highly intelligent great ape.

The problem of course with such pictures of gorilla expressions is that it is easy to get all anthropomorphic and try to relate them to human society. An image of a gorilla appearing to smile is probably not smiling at all but showing a "fear grin". A silverback pouting his lips could be a warning of an impending charge. For these reasons I thought long and hard about including this gallery here. In the end I decided that this would be a great way of connecting you, the reader, with mountain gorillas. If one of my images makes you smile, or even if it makes you or your kids pull the same face, then my plan has worked. You are not ridiculing the gorilla by doing this, instead I have made you think about mountain gorillas and the next time you see something about their conservation, hopefully you will want to do something to help.

The image on the left shows a very relaxed blackback that sat in front of my group for ages watching us. Blackbacks are silverbacks-in-waiting, i.e they are mature males below 10 years of age that have yet to develop the sheer bulk and other attributes of a silverback. They are usually very relaxed individuals and this one was no exception. I have always loved the gentle feel to this image.

The larger image opposite is a female in the Hirwa group. We found the whole lot laying together in a mass of black fur, with Lucky fast asleep at the back. In fact all slept, except one old female who watched us intently for the whole of our visit. Every move was watched with interest with unblinking eyes. I've said it before, but I do feel that gorillas watch us as much as we watch them.

Ever wondered how we can tell one mountain gorilla from another? Well the late Dian Fossey faced the same problem and devised a unique way of telling them apart – by their nose prints. Just like our fingerprints, a gorilla nose print is unique and no two are the same. There are few images in this book that show direct eye contact with a silverback. Body language is all important to gorillas and the silverback may consider extended eye contact a challenge. When Akarevuro fixed me with this stare I took one shot, put the camera down and made it obvious that I was averting my eyes away from him.

Mountain gorillas have 32 teeth, the same number as humans, and they are mainly molars used for grinding down food. The canines are used primarily for defence and also for crushing tough stems like bamboo. In 2007, a research team found a set of 9 teeth that were reported to be 10 million years old and virtually indistinguishable from the teeth of modern day gorillas.

And just for the record, this silverback wasn't doing anything aggressive... he was just yawning as he had literally just woken up!

Sleep my friend and dream of a world that loves its mountain gorillas.

SUSA GROUP
Gorillas in the clouds

Susa group is the holy grail for the serious gorilla tourist. Located on the slopes of the steep Karisimbi Volcano, the attraction of Susa has always been the sheer group size (once 39 individuals, now 29 due to a recent split) and the fact that the late Dian Fossey studied them. Susa are the highest group of mountain gorillas in Rwanda; you can easily trek beyond 10,000 ft before finding them. This would make *Gorillas in the Clouds* a much better film title than *Gorillas in the Mist* I think, don't you? It is this feeling of being on top of the world with gorillas, together with the incredible habitat, that has always attracted me to Susa.

My first visit to them was very special. I will gloss over the walk if I may, suffice it to say that it took two relentless hours at a very steep angle just to get to the wall; the rain was horizontal from the start as well, oh deep joy. The oxygen got noticeably thinner too and several of my group had mild headaches and tingling fingers during the climb. At about 9500 ft, completely drenched through, we reached the wall. The gorillas were 'at least' another hours climb and we pushed our weary bodies onwards.

Over the wall the vegetation changed completely from what I expected. Usually I see bamboo or hypericum forest but this was afromontane rainforest; the Lobelias were incredible. Lichens literally dripped from everywhere, the mist clung spookily to the tops of the forest and all was lush and green. I would have made the climb just to see the forest it was so cool. Any tree hugger dreams were suddenly interrupted by the sight of black shapes moving in the clearing above. I often wish that I have more time to take landscapes but when you are on a gorilla trek, time is precious and landscapes have to be snapshots.

We reached the gorillas just as the mist descended even more; it was like Halloween in the Virungas. The rain thankfully turned to drizzle, which kept the gorillas out of the jungle. Nothing is grumpier than a soaking wet gorilla, trust me on that one.

We found the dominant silverback Kurira almost straight away; he was stretched out sleeping at the edge of the jungle. He looked so peaceful and I am sure he would have stayed that way for the whole visit. Unfortunately a youngster had other ideas and rolled straight down the hill into his side. With a stifled groan he sat up, the youngster taking it as an opportunity to jump on his huge domed head! Gently he pushed the little guy off; they really are so tolerant of the little ones who can get away with almost anything. Then he stood up, stretched and walked to the ridge just above us.

He looked out over his domain, a proud animal in his kingdom in the clouds. Surrounded by the lush vegetation, this is one of my favourite silverback shots. In fact, it is one of my all time favourite mountain gorilla shots.

As if on command, gorillas started emerging from every bush. More and more kept coming and soon it was difficult to know which way to look. To be in the middle of a large group of mountain gorillas is always a very special experience and one for which Susa is famous. Photographing this of course is impossible, as trees and bushes are always in the wrong place!

I always keep an eye on the silverback as he is usually the centre of attention, but this time it was a female that really caught my eye. She had a really playful youngster and they were having a lot of fun. I watched as she gently tickled the little one, his happy chuckling was infectious and soon my grin was just as wide.

Gorillas are great sleepers and spend around 40% of their time in some kind of resting position. As our visit drew to a close, the time approached for their midday siesta. Groups of gorillas were bedding down to sleep everywhere I looked. The silverback was in the centre of the pile, with the mothers in very close proximity. Even the youngsters got the message after a while and suddenly the jungle was quiet. The Susa group had been wonderful to us. It was time to leave the gorillas in the clouds to their siesta, so reluctantly we headed for home.

GROWING UP
New life new hope

One of the ultimate pleasures of being a wildlife photographer, is when a mother trusts you enough to let you see what is most precious to her in her world. A newborn mountain gorilla is perhaps more special than most, as their numbers are so small. Every new mountain gorilla life is incredibly precious and a success for all who strive to protect them. The first newborn I ever saw was in the Hirwa group. Mothers at this stage are very protective and usually stay in close proximity to the silverback for protection. This mother was no exception and sat right next to Lucky. For a few fleeting seconds, I caught sight of a tiny foot sticking out from her fur, until a great black bulk blocked out everything. Lucky the silverback had deliberately moved to block my view; it was a deliberate protective act for the newborn and I respected him for it.

About halfway through the encounter, the mother moved to one side and deliberately turned to face our group. She was cradling something in her arms and I realised that she was intentionally showing us her baby. At first I couldn't see the youngster, then a tiny hand appeared in her fur, followed by a tiny face. The eyes were barely open it was so young.

The next 5 minutes I will remember forever. The female looked straight at me and moved the baby in her arms so that I could see it. She looked at me again and I tried to appear as passive as possible. I watch transfixed as she cradled the baby in her arms, tenderly fussing over it before gently kissing each tiny foot. As I write this now I am welling up with emotion; at the time I remember being totally overwhelmed. When I looked, every one of my fellow trekkers and the guide were watching with great big smiles on their faces. Some were crying and I admit that I probably was too. It was an incredible moment of pure tenderness and her eyes said more than any words could. Like any human mother she was so proud of her baby, you could see the love from her and she wanted to share it with us. That is the trust that mountain gorillas show in us.

Another tender moment from the 'Bad Hair Day' encounter earlier in this book. It's alarmingly anthropomorphic to say this but I could see little difference between the female gorilla and a human parent. She was attentive, incredibly patient, playful, protective and clearly bursting with love. She was everything that a mother should be. Whilst I am not attempting to make them sound human in anyway, even though there is only 2% difference in our DNA, perhaps we do need to start thinking of them as our close cousins and not just wild animals.

🌿 Mountain gorillas breast feed their youngsters for up to three years, which coincides with the infant's development of its second set of teeth. After about 8-9 months the youngsters are eating vegetation too, but are still dependent on the milk.

🌿 A female will not give birth until at least 10 years of age and on average she will wait until her young are independent (3.5 - 4 years) before breeding again. This means that mountain gorillas have a very slow rate of reproduction, one reason why every new birth is so special.

⸱⸱⸱⋗ With each successful tree climb, the youngsters get bolder. Whilst mountain gorillas are good climbers, experienced trekkers never stand underneath them as it can be dangerous. Although they undoubtedly have climbing prowess, their judgement of the weight bearing ability of branches sometimes needs a little fine tuning. This little chap was perfectly safe on his branch and was swinging on the tree for five minutes before launching a flying attack on another one below.

As youngsters get older, their confidence grows and they start to explore their surroundings a little more. I came across this little one in Group 13. The mother was feeding on the ground below and this tree must have looked exciting. Slowly the youngster climbed up until the trees became too far apart for little legs. Not quite sure what to do next, the youngster tried various combinations of his feet and hands to solve the problem without success. The mother watched from below, I guess keen to let the youngster learn by itself. Eventually it figured out that the best way down was to grab the thickest branch; lesson learnt for that day!

For the first few months of life young mountain gorillas are too small and fragile to cope with the demands of the Virungas. Steep slopes, tough vegetation and the constant movement whilst feeding are too much for little legs. So, whenever the female moves, she hoists the youngster on her back or around her neck so it can hitch a ride. To me it always looks as if the youngster clings on for dear life!

Mountain gorillas eat a wide variety of plant species. Like humans they have a single stomach, which is inefficient for digesting vegetation. They compensate for this by eating large amounts of food per day, over 20 kg for a silverback. It's great fun to watch them stripping away the outside of shoots to get to the tender juicy part inside, this little chap was really enjoying himself too!

Mountain gorillas also eat ants and youngsters learn the hard way to eat quickly. I watched as this one dug down to the ant nest and pulled up an arm full of ants. They were eaten quickly before the arm went back down for more. One of his siblings wasn't quite as experienced and ran off chattering and scratching everywhere as the ants started to bite. We were all bitten too, especially my girlfriend Carol who had to strip down to her underwear to get rid of her little army of admirers. I didn't see the trackers complaining though. I think it made their day!

ONE BAMBOO TOO MANY

An unforgettable experience

Every visit to a mountain gorilla group is unique and just when I think I have seen it all, they always manage to surprise me again. I have had some spectacular experiences with the 'All Action Kwitonda' group, but nothing could have prepared me for the bizarre events that were about to unfold before my eyes that day.

After a very easy trek with our guide Edward, we found the silverback Kwitonda in a thick bamboo forest. He was sitting back munching a fresh bamboo cane and all around him were the results of the feast. In fact when I looked closely, there were chewed bamboo canes everywhere; clearly they had been eating a lot of bamboo. All around us the bushes were vibrating with youngsters and adults in full play; they all seemed exceptionally happy. One of the youngsters came bounding out of the forest and started running around a small tree like it was a maypole. Round and round the little chap went, holding on all the time and sporting what looked like an insane grin. He continued this for several minutes, making little noises all the time, until eventually he just collapsed on the floor and lay there watching us. Clearly they were all in a VERY good mood.

We moved on and soon came across Akarevuro, the apprentice silverback, standing unusually on his hind legs. It was unusual on two counts – firstly because gorillas spend most of their time on their bottoms or on all fours and secondly, because he wasn't exactly walking... but more like he was staggering. I kid you not; I had to pinch myself to believe it. He grabbed a bamboo cane for support, broke it and immediately grabbed another handful before he fell over. Reading the situation, our guide Edward backed us well away. Something was up with Akarevuro; he certainly wasn't behaving like any mountain gorilla I had ever seen before. He pulled himself upright again, lurched in our general direction then crashed off into the jungle. I have seen that same behaviour on many nights out in the UK, but never in the Virungas. Something was clearly up.

:: We turned our attention to a blackback that was munching through some freshly stripped bamboo. "Look there quick" said Edward and I followed his pointing figure. Akarevuro had reappeared and was headed straight for the blackback. A slap around the head announced his presence. Instead of running away, the blackback stood up and started bear hugging the young silverback. Huh, what was happening? For 15 minutes they wrestled like this, using some pretty smart moves I might add, flattening bushes and trees all around.

Every so often they would break the bear hug, separate and then charge at each other beating their chests. It was a pure adrenaline rush but we made sure that we kept our distance, as there was a lot of weight being thrown around. They were also chattering to each other all the time. I am not a gorilla expert but they sounded very excited to me. It is one thing to watch two youngsters play fighting, but to see two adult mountain gorillas pounding into each other was awe inspiring.

After 15 minutes of constant wrestling, both of them were clearly exhausted and sat down. The play continued even then, until the blackback gave up and stumbled off into the forest. In the ensuing silence, I could hear the crashing of bushes all around; other gorillas must have been playing too. In my limited experience, mountain gorillas just don't behave like this normally, something must have induced it.

Our time was up and so ended one of the most amazing hours that I have ever had with mountain gorillas. Now I have a theory about what might have caused their behaviour. I am not a scientist or gorilla expert, just someone who is really experienced with wildlife in the field. The gorillas had been eating a lot of bamboo cane; the discarded shoots were everywhere. I had certainly seen Kwitonda munching his way through a stack right at the start. It is common knowledge that certain fermenting fruits and tree sap, in the right conditions, can induce an alcoholic effect. There are numerous films about elephants and other wildlife getting a little tipsy on over-ripe fruits like marula. Putting two and two together, I wonder if the fermenting bamboo sap was the source of all the high jinks? Of course I am not going to suggest for one moment that the Kwitonda group like a drink or two, but maybe… just maybe the bamboo sap had an effect. I guess we will never know for sure but if I were a detective, I would say that all the evidence pointed to the fact that fermented bamboo played a part…

GORILLA TOURISM AND CONSERVATION

The key to success

The main threats to gorillas are poaching, habitat loss through mining or deforestation and regional conflicts. In some areas, the effects of these are devastating to the local gorilla population; in particular illegal mining in the Democratic Republic of Congo. The main threat to mountain gorillas is that 90% of the locals make their living from subsistence (cash crop) farming. Therefore, they see the gorillas as direct competition to their livelihoods, which is how conflicts can occur.

The image shown here is more than just a bag of potatoes. It shows the problem of mountain gorilla conservation in Rwanda. In the foreground, the bags of potatoes provide the main income for locals who harvest them. Immediately behind that are the potato fields, which would have been pristine forest and prime gorilla habitat a few years ago. In the distance just behind the wall, the jungle starts and this is where the mountain gorillas call home. Of course it is too late to protect the forest in front of the wall, but it is now vital to protect what they have left of the forest behind that boundary. The key to this is to convince the locals that it is in their best interests to conserve and protect the mountain gorillas and in return, they receive additional income or gain quality of life by doing so. This is where sustainable tourism can help and to tell you more about this, who better than Will Bolsover, Managing Director of World Primate Safaris.

TOURISM – SAINT OR SINNER?

One of the most controversial topics associated with wildlife conservation is often tourism. Who does it benefit... the wildlife or the tourists? I know it's a tricky question but personally it's one I think mountain gorillas answer quite succinctly.

Mountain gorillas have been highly endangered for a number of years and live in one of the most restricted habitats left on the planet today. Surrounded by human encroachment, these apes have surprisingly defied all odds and in recent years, their population has actually increased. Of course the dedicated work of researchers, forest staff and conservation organisations is a major contribution to this, but undoubtedly so is tourism. The mountain gorillas of Rwanda are living, breathing (but not talking!) proof of tourism and conservation working together in unity.

Mountain gorilla tourism is big business for the Central and East African countries of Rwanda, Uganda and the DRC; the DRC, due to political instability, is still in the early stages of gorilla tourism, however Rwanda and Uganda are reaping the benefits. The success of these two mountain gorilla destinations, and Rwanda in particular, is all the more evident when you look at the finances. One gorilla permit to track gorillas for one hour costs USD$500. This means that during the average lifespan of a gorilla of 30 years it could generate approximately USD$44million.

Figures such as this are hard to ignore. You may even say to yourself that this is an awful lot of money to be generated just to save some hairy apes in some distant mountains... well you would be wrong. Vast sums of money are required on a daily, monthly and annual basis in order to protect and conserve this endangered species. It is the money that is generated from the sale of these gorilla permits that helps to do this. This money contributes towards the maintenance of the park boundaries, medical assistance for both the gorillas and the local population and also to support the local residents, who are now not permitted to make use of the resources of the local forest. Importantly, it is also used to pay the salaries of the park staff and rangers who patrol this region on a daily basis monitoring the gorillas and ensuring that those people that are not meant to be in the park... are not there.

To put this in a very simple context, over 100 park rangers in the last 10 years have lost their lives whilst protecting mountain gorillas. For this reason alone, the finance that the sale of these gorilla permits generates is essential in order to continue to support the various conservation initiatives and local communities of this region that all contribute to the survival of these gentle giants.

So how does sustainable tourism fit into this? Well, firstly, it can only work if the local communities benefit from gorilla tourism and its associated revenues, and are involved from the beginning. This involvement, both financially and emotionally, is the lynch pin in the success of gorilla conservation. Without the support of these communities, mountain gorillas would have vanished off the face of the Earth years ago. These communities have often had their livelihoods changed in order to make way for saving an endangered species; forests that were once there to be hunted and trees that were there to be chopped for firewood are suddenly no longer accessible to these people and for this reason, they must be compensated. This compensation comes in the form of jobs created by the tourism trade whether it be in construction, guiding, working in lodges or even local dance troupes; this all contributes to the survival of the community. Too often in the past have the needs of neighbouring human communities been overlooked in order to save an endangered animal, which only results in tension and conflict. In order for conservation and also eco-tourism to work, it must work to the benefit of all involved and that includes the local human population as well as the wildlife. It is through the means mentioned here, and also with the assistance of the Rwandan Government and the tourism board (ORTPN), that Rwanda is home to a burgeoning economy at the same time as conserving some of the most critically endangered apes left on our planet.

The reasons mentioned above also illustrate how essential the role of reputable gorilla safari operators is in the conservation of mountain gorillas. Here at World Primate Safaris, we try to support eco-friendly lodges in the region that in turn support local community projects. At all times, we try to employ local people and only work with local operators who are conscientious in their employment of staff and those that have knowledgeable and friendly guides. All of these contributing factors ensure that the visiting tourist receives a fun and educational experience, as well as directly contributing to the local community and economy.

Of course tourism is not all good, and this must be taken into consideration whenever planning a gorilla safari. Rules and regulations must be followed at all times; a strict 7 metre viewing distance is essential, firstly not to pass on any human illnesses to our amiable cousins as even a common cold could wipe out an entire gorilla family just like that, and secondly not to unduly stress them. Any reputable safari operator will make these points clear from the outset and ensure that they are followed to the letter whilst on the ground.

In my humble opinion, the presence of tourists in the national park contributes positively to the daily monitoring of the various mountain gorilla groups as well as discouraging the small minority of people that pose a significant threat to the gorillas, such as poachers. I can honestly say that I am a firm believer that if tourism to see the gorillas had not been commenced – as certain high profile personalities such as Dian Fossey

understandably at the time did not originally want – then mountain gorillas would not be in existence today. We do however owe a huge debt of gratitude to the likes of George Schaller and Dian Fossey. If it had not been for these pioneers in great ape conservation, then we would in all likelihood not have understood the threats facing mountain gorillas in time. These renowned conservationists dedicated their lives to the survival of these great apes, and through this, brought their plight to the attention of the world. Nowadays, following in the footsteps of Fossey and her colleagues, are a number of gorilla conservation organisations that successfully dedicate their time, money, and efforts to the survival of mountain gorillas in their natural habitat.

In summary, it is fair to say that money is a powerful motivator and as a result of the success of eco-tourism and conservation working together, these affable apes are a major contributor to one of the fastest growing economies in Africa, that of Rwanda. A country that has been through more than we can imagine, Rwanda, also known as the Land of a Thousand Hills, is hospitable beyond comprehension and offers a unique wildlife experience that is at the top of the list of most enthusiasts. By visiting the mountain gorillas, you are making a positive contribution to their conservation and also ensuring that local communities benefit too.

Although throughout this text we discuss a "conservation success", there is still a long way to go. Mountain gorilla numbers are still worryingly low and their habitat is forever being encroached upon. The last refuge of the mountain gorillas is still under threat and as long as this is the case, eco-tourism and conservation efforts must continue...

Will Bolsover
www.worldprimatesafaris.com

CONSERVATION IN ACTION

A day in the life of a Gorilla Doctor

The Mountain Gorilla Veterinary Project (MGVP) oversee the health of all mountain gorillas and also of anyone that works with them. This *One Health* approach guarantees (as much as is possible with wild animals) that mountain gorillas are protected from human diseases that could wipe them out. Therefore they perform a vital role in the conservation of the mountain gorilla which is why they are beneficiaries from the donations made by this book. Jan, their Field Director, tells us more about their work.

A day in the life of a Gorilla Doctor

For Gorilla Doctors there is really no typical day! We plan out each week in detail, and then go with the flow, letting the gorillas dictate our time. The Mountain Gorilla Veterinary Project is a regional team of 12 veterinarians based in Musanze, Rwanda, with offices in the Democratic Republic of Congo (DRC) and Uganda. We provide medical care for all of the habituated mountain gorillas in the world. Our days are filled with routine health checks, interventions to remove snares or dart with life saving antibiotics, treating orphaned gorillas, vaccinating dogs against rabies, and coordinating human health care programs for all trackers and guides in Rwanda and DRC.

Mornings begin early on days we go to the forest for a routine visual check of one of the habituated groups. It is still dark when we get up, and by 6 a.m. we're headed for the edge of the park. With advance trackers, Gorilla Doctors head up the mountain, tracking gorillas up and down until we find them. We mark the position with GPS, and then try to get our eyes on every gorilla in the group, making sure there is no illness or injury. Then we head back down the mountain to write our reports – yes, even here we have paperwork!

When we get a report of a sick or injured gorilla that is in need of medical intervention, we quickly gather our team, check our forest bags, and with experienced trackers head to the group in question. If darting is necessary, we wait for the perfect shot, and with the dart gun hidden behind a tracker (gorillas know what the gun is so we must hide it!) we dart the selected gorilla, hoping that the silverback does not get too upset. Trackers then form a perimeter around the sleeping gorilla, keeping the silverback and other group members away using voices or hitting the ground with sticks. Once we are finished with our work we wake up the gorilla, and reunite it with the group.

Some days are quiet, and we get the required desk work done, but we are always prepared for that call that requires us to scramble to help a gorilla, whether it is in Rwanda, DRC or Uganda, wild or orphan. We're here, on call, 24/7!

For more information visit:
www.gorilladoctors.org

Mountain gorilla trekking is a great experience. You get to hike in stunning surroundings, see the last mountain gorillas and benefit conservation too. Don't expect a morning lie in, gorilla treks start very early. After a short briefing at Gorilla HQ you are assigned to your gorilla group and then it's off with your porters and guide for your trek. It can take between 1 and 4 hours to reach each gorilla group; the walk varies between easy and absolute hell. You don't have to be a mountain climber to complete a gorilla trek but you do have to be fit (especially for the Stairway to Heaven Susa group). All of our clients prepare for their treks a few months in advance, as we generally run longer tours than most. When you reach the gorillas, you'll get another quick briefing from your guide, meet the trackers, dump all your food and then it's off for the experience of a lifetime. After one hour you are finished, and for both Will and I, the next 23 hours cannot pass quick enough until the next trek.

Will's top tips for mountain gorilla trekking are to ensure that you do more than one trek (since it is so awesome) and to put your camera down sometimes and just watch. When you plan your trip, hopefully with World Primate Safaris, please try to see more of Rwanda than the Virungas; the Land of a Thousand Hills has so much to offer. Some opportunities not to be missed include the beautiful montane forest of Nyungwe where you can track chimpanzees, black and white Colobus monkeys and also enjoy the local tea plantations, or alternatively explore the beautiful Akagera National Park, an up and coming savannah game experience that offers a great overview of this stunning Land of a Thousand Hills.

My top tip (apart from photography which is dealt with later) is to always respect your guides, trackers and porters. Your guides are vital for explaining gorilla behaviour and being your link to the mountain gorillas, and it's your porters that carry your heavy gear up those slopes. But it's the trackers that I always pay special attention to as they get forgotten. These guys leave at first light in the morning to find the gorillas for you to track, help you during the visit then stay with them until dark that day to ensure their safety. They are the front line of gorilla conservation. One of my friends Majoro Emanuel (shown with me above) is one of the trackers for my favourite silverback Lucky. His face always lights up with a broad grin when I arrive and I have built a very friendly relationship with him. I am telling you this so that you will be nice to your trackers, tip them well and give them some water or a chocolate bar; trust me they will appreciate it. It also gives a good impression of tourists to them, which in turn helps all of us save the mountain gorilla.

Both Will and I are addicted to mountain gorilla trekking and supporting their conservation by sustainable tourism. If you have been inspired by this book to come on one of my expeditions, or perhaps go with family or friends, then please contact Will at World Primate Safaris using the details shown on page 96.

PHOTO NOTES
Getting great shots

Gorillas appeal to the soul and I hope that some of the photographs in this book have triggered an emotional response within you. I have witnessed on numerous occasions, the effect that seeing gorillas has had on people, especially photographers. I have seen clients with little confidence and rudimentary camera equipment take pictures well beyond their expectations. Although I would like to take credit for this, in reality it is simply a reaction to the amazing feeling of being face to face with our close cousins. Gorillas exude calm when you are with them and this clearly convinces photographers to slow down and take their time; a lesson for everyone I think.

I hope that you have enjoyed the photographs in this book as much as I have been inspired to take them. Mountain gorillas really challenge my photography and continually push my abilities to the limit. I am constantly working at the edge of what is technically possible, since light levels are low on the slopes of the Virungas. Of course, they are low because I choose to always shoot under the cloud cover during the rainy season in Rwanda. On a technical level, this is to reduce unflattering shadows on the face and to keep the dynamic range between the dark gorilla and the sky manageable. Aesthetically there is something romantic about gorillas living on the misty, moody slopes of a volcano. I absolutely hate images of gorillas taken in the sunlight; for me, they just lack something.

Working with such low light conditions and handholding the camera dictates that the shutter speed must be kept high to reduce camera shake. I always set the ISO these days at a minimum of 800 to achieve this, a setting that has been made possible by using a Nikon D3s. This camera has revolutionised my mountain gorilla photography, allowing me to really express myself without compromise.

One refreshing benefit of photographing mountain gorillas is that I do not have to carry tons of gear around the world. Most of the images taken in this book were with either a 70-200mm lens or shorter, some were even with a compact. Gorilla photography is well within the realms of anyone. Always remember that sometimes you will only return with a handful of images, but always with a lifetime of memories.

The cute appeal

We are all softies for the cute shot and there is nothing wrong with that! Just keep the shot simple with the story completely on the youngster. With this shot I could have included the mother, but it would have rendered the baby very small in the final image and it would have been lost in the background. So I opted for a tighter shot and just gave an impression of the mother being there... and it worked!

Great people portraits

Rwanda is so much more than a home for mountain gorillas. The people are wonderful and several lodges have professional troupes of colourful Intore dancers. They are great subjects for photography and will add to your Rwandan experience. Try to arrange to photograph them at the end of the day when the light is best, as this will help with skin tones and ensure that there are no harsh shadows. At the end of your photography, please make a donation to the group. It sends a good message and helps build sustainable tourism.

Telling a story

It's so easy to just take portraits when you go gorilla trekking as the subject is so willing! Whilst there is space in everyone's portfolio for compelling portraits, don't forget to take a wider view that tells a better story. With this image the story is obvious. In the foreground you can see a group of gorillas, the silverback is asleep on the left. In the middle distance you can see where the forest meets the farmland. The story here is simply of how close mountain gorillas are to human habitation and it graphically shows the pressure on their habitat. To take images like this I always have one camera attached to a wide-angle lens, in this case a 24-70mm. I have the aperture set to f11 to give a decent depth of field. Telling a conservation or behavioural story via the medium of photography is a skill that all photographers need to learn. It will make your pictures more interesting for those at home.

Compelling portraits

Good portraits need to have a degree of eye contact to show a connection between photographer and gorilla. The main obstacle to overcome with any gorilla portrait are the deep shadows over their eyes created by their large eye ridges. The only way to get around this, since the usage of flash is rightly prohibited, is to photograph under diffuse skies and to wait until your subject looks up. Muninya is always an easy portrait subject as he tends to look up, thus revealing his eyes. To get this portrait I used an aperture of f11 (which necessitated an ISO of 1000 on the Nikon D3s) and selected an autofocus point that was right between the eyes. Using my 70-200mm lens with a 1.4x teleconverter gave me the compression effect I needed to create the portrait. Muninya did the rest.

Use the habitat

Gorillas live in a beautiful forest environment that literally screams out to be included in any photograph. The fresh green foliage and lush lichens add much needed colour and provide a lovely contrast to the dark tones of the gorilla. With this image I wanted to show a young, independent gorilla in the context of its forest home. So I used a technique called a Look-Thru to illustrate this. With my eye looking through the camera viewfinder, I moved around until I found a hole in the vegetation close to the camera through which I could clearly see the gorilla. At a low aperture of f4 and with the focus on the gorilla, the foreground vegetation became very diffuse in the shot and formed a natural frame around the subject. A lovely technique that always produces great results.

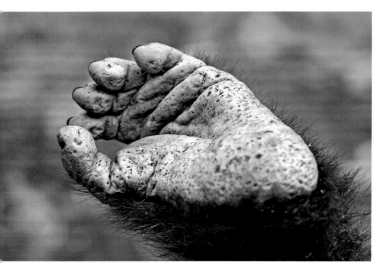

Photo © Sue Earnshaw

Look for detail

When I put this book together with Eddie Ephraums it really challenged me to find images that were different from the usual gorilla shots. I found many in my database like this one, that would never see the light of day in a commercial world but which showed an interesting viewpoint on a part of the gorilla's anatomy. In this case it was the heavily marked foot of an old female gorilla, stuck straight in the air whilst she was totally asleep. I really loved the rough patterns and detail on the foot, so used the 70-200mm lens with the 1.4 converter, combined with a low aperture of f4, to throw the background out of focus and only have a small part of the foot sharp too. Here's a challenge for you. Try to get the silvery stripe on the back of a silverback. It's amazing!

Look for landscapes

The Rwandan landscape is beautiful to photograph as I hope that you have seen in this book. If you are presenting a portfolio of work, perhaps for a competition, an award or just to show friends, then showing the landscape of the Virunga Volcanoes is a must have. The problem is that the volcanoes are often under low cloud, or it's difficult to get the right access. I always carry a compact camera with me for just such occasions. To get this landscape, I leant out of the vehicle on our way back from the local cultural village. I was much the worse for wear after drinking far too much banana beer and it's a wonder that I got anything in the frame!

Gear

For the vast majority of images in this book, I used the Nikon D3, D3s and D3x DSLRs. All images were shot in RAW. Lenses were usually a 70-200 f2.8 VR with a 1.4x teleconverter and a 24-70mm lens. Compacts were either the Canon G10 or the Nikon P7000. All images were processed in either NX2 or Photoshop and retain the spirit of the original RAW image. I always wear clothes from Paramo Directional Clothing Systems as they are perfect for the tough environment of the Virungas; they are ethically manufactured and are my partners in a conservation fund.

I make no apologies for the hat!

RWANDA

In the Introduction to this book, I mention that Rwanda is perceived as a dangerous country to visit. In my opinion, and I suspect the opinion of every single tourist that visits Rwanda, it is one of the nicest countries in Africa. In fact it's a very pleasant surprise. The first thing that strikes you when driving away from the airport in Kigali is the cleanliness. There is no litter anywhere. The second thing you notice are the smiles that are almost everywhere. It's a beautiful, clean and safe country where both Will and I feel very much at home.

Rwanda has a rapidly expanding population and there are children everywhere. They are the future of Rwanda and into their hands will pass the collective responsibility for mountain gorilla conservation. It is my hope that this new generation will know nothing of the old days, and that local communities will understand the benefits of living alongside mountain gorillas. Moreover, mountain gorillas will be considered an essential part of Rwandan life. Then, and only then, mountain gorillas may be safe from the unforgiving embrace of extinction. Until then they need our continued protection to survive.

I would like to dedicate this book to the following:

To all my clients who have made my dreams a reality, sorry for pushing you so hard up those slopes!

To the nameless rangers, park staff and trackers who risk their lives every day to protect these endangered mountain gorillas. You will never be forgotten.

To Will, work colleague and friend, I told you we could do it!

To Dad, we will never forget Mum.

And finally to Carol, for always being there when I need a hug and for diligently editing this book.

I would also like to offer special thanks to the following:

Will Bolsover and all at World Primate Safaris, Prosper Uwingeli and his guides – Edward, Diogene and Olivier, drivers – John, Shema and Musa who have helped me through these years, Jan and all at the MGVP, my agent Tim Harris for encouraging my gorilla project, Ed at Rex for helping to gain worldwide press exposure for mountain gorillas, Ian Redmond OBE, Veronika Lenarz, Mark Carwardine, Leon and all at Butler Tanner & Dennis for making the production of this book so easy and all my Facebook fans who helped me choose the cover for this book.

And as always Eddie Ephraums, mentor, designer, friend and fellow café lover, I could not have done this without your help.

If you have been inspired by this book and want to come on one of my safaris or expeditions, or to arrange your own adventure, then please contact Will Bolsover as below

World Primate Safaris
Tel: 0044 (0) 1273 691 642
US Toll Free: 1866 357 6569
sales@worldprimatesafaris.com
www.worldprimatesafaris.com

I hope that you have enjoyed this journey into the life of the mountain gorilla. Here's how to find out more about my expeditions, recent pictures, talks, merchandise and my awful sense of humour:

www.andyrouse.co.uk
Facebook fan page: www.facebook.com/andyrousephoto

First published in Great Britain 2011
by Electric Squirrel Publishing
Studio 10, Apex House, Trethomas, Glamorgan, CF83 8DP, UK
www.andyrouse.co.uk

Copyright © Andy Rouse 2011

Andy Rouse has asserted his right to be identified as the author of this work in accordance with the Copyright, Designs and Patents Act 1988.

A catalogue record for this book is available from the British Library.

ISBN 978-0-9564575-1-6

Design and production by Eddie Ephraums
www.envisagebooks.co.uk

Printed and bound by Butler, Tanner & Dennis, UK